Oven Heat & Sunlight

poems from the Mystic Mother

Markus Adam

Copyright © 2019 Markus Adam

ISBN:9781095586853

Dedicated to my mom and to all mothers

PROLOGUE

i invent your voice
i connect the secrets of your body
slowly you rise
pore by pore
mole by mole
until the browns and tans
catch your skin
and the
sensual grains of dust
that were once unborn
and unimportant
gather to
adorn your hips with themselves

creation
from adoration

a
hot tongue
in the
mouth of a virgin

1

To whom the universe is exhaling
i offer the fetus of divinity
like a sensual potter
uniting flesh and spirit

within the mortal vessel of woman
i mold a cradle
where sand and sea meet
where form and vapour
are ingested
and
blessed

to each limb i inscribe a vein
a trace of life linking the essence
to its source
              wormwood in deep bark
imprints of an underwater
              current
all are signatures of nature
and as the breath of the sky
weaves through a thick forest
the blood of my creation
courses beneath

2

well the sun has dragged itself down once again
    and the birth of night is now labouring

drinking gin with Miles Davis on a cool approach
and the swing of horns swelling

oh how i wish my guitar would mold into a fleshy
woman to ease me into midnight

        the room seems a universe of awe

where are you

woman of a thousand faces

woman of an alpine meadow

hiding with the small grass blades

        breathing a low whisper

coax and moan while i gaze over you

looking for a path

to your wavy bed

from here you seem less real

from here i can see an ocean in foam

        a desert in heat

and i ache for your surreal attempt to
        signal my approach

poetry is a hot tongue in the mouth of a virgin

poetry is the smell of friction between lovers'
bellies

poetry is the gaze of a newborn child

poetry is not the words on a page

3

prairie thin winds whisper
through a rustling pane
beside this dreamers head
settled in a strange woman's
room
with passing guitars
and a simple moon blanketed
couch
he wants nothing to last
like the invisible turning of the seasons

4

i kneel at your bosom
under a shower
rowing across the glides
of our future children

bending over separate
arches i walk barefoot
through the moles of
wood bark
like a sweating steed

hands and morals wreathe
beyond pleasure
surely sounding
they become lovers
in ensured trust
and tend to the fire
of our hearts

5

i'm a man who would let your eyes
be discovered
by another
abroad
with jellyfish and crystal shells

and after you are domestic
and resemble marble idols
i will tell how my voice
was the spirit in hearts
that were moved
towards your irises

will you give to me the rose of your love
and leave me dancing in the shadow of an orange
moon
between
trees
with resembling skin
who have ears for sacred songs
which hymn
and grace
flood after a dusk rain
just a rose my simple one
so that i may have
something to look upon you with

now that time knows of our embrace
the day must come when
we shall meet
and although night has since dipped its brush
into the brew of our love
the last stroke across the moon still
aches
in yearning beyond the wide pale
horizon

but
aloft on that brilliant summit
a soft melody covered in the pink blanket of dawn
issues like a young rose
reaching for the acceptance of the blessing sun

7

the music is heat
            for the exhibitionist
      in front of the
      mirror

her legs made my torso
      hip about
my legs were wrapped
  and sullen

then her neck would bring pythons
into my neck
and my neck swooned

her fingers would
light my skin
while
my fingers
conducted
our maelstrom

8

mist rises over swaddled stems of grass
caught by night and
her misty cloak
called in wide shadowy hymns
by the stream below

your thigh is
slightly lifted to my lowered head
calm in sweetgrass spread bravely
through the hills

night embroiders us within her woven symmetry of
simplicity and the solitude of beauty unfurls
gently upon us

soiled lovers
embraced by a
single
darkened stem
waiting for our call
from the star freckled stream
below

9

i don't want your woman
i only want her love

10

i must write on love
others have and they soon died
i do not wish to perish without writing this now
i love you and pursue you with that in mind
who you are i need not know
what i know is that i love you
i have loved others and through them
i loved you
for you i blessed their skin
for you i soothed their pains
within them was your soul
each blossom of our love i placed with your image
my love for you was on the sweetness of each word
within each earthy kiss
you are the wetness of passion
the soft core of delight
and how i dream each night in the womb of your
distance

time withholds you in jealousy and i must write
this now
before it devours me

i only wish to love another

to love you

11

sweet woman

your form outlasts thought

and settles as an unknown fragrance behind

my eyes

i am guided by this instinct

yet

i pursue in forgotten purpose your same form

all reminiscences

memories

of

feeling

your imprint on my structure

is a universe of laws

and predestined patterns

i

construct

you

with

12

i give her a bath of words
scrub her with
paragraphs soaked
in mellow dashes
and soft floating
apostrophes

i like my exclamation point
or is it
a question mark
she raises when
her comma is
connecting our verbs

silent vowels arch to
the moon
when she hyphens
her short breaths
into our active phrase

she needs me period
but i abbreviate
my oration and
drift behind a semi-colon's
                    aching promise

13

you left your brown skin in my bed
hair threaded
i woke to its stirring
your face on the pillow
i moved towards your scent
drawn
like ancient shapes
this jungle moves into reminders
of breath
and breathing
the winds still parting from our movement
and colours too unfamiliar
to be called
home
your exotic
brown skin
a new ceremony
for my
prairie heart

14

before i slide back into eternity's sheath
i will taste and spread your nectar
across the legends of my swirling cosmos

even if i arrive crawling at your barren oasis
i will drink the whispers of you
dying with each scorched pebble
to be scattered in sacred resurrections of your
sublime form
at which i worship
as your moon
or moons
in love
or in garments of alchemy
forever tracing the scent of your disappearance

you are an unshared treasure
spawning seekers
and spurning gods
who accept no prayers
or price
for the naming of your starry brew of
wildcraft
and
meadows

the herbs of your becoming

spread far and

beyond the

blade of my wanting

the smell of friction
between
lovers' bellies

15

darling
i wrote you into my soul
in times of certainty
how limited they were
now
in this air of indecision
i may write you out of my verbal heart

darling call this not a change of heart
but a revolt of consideration
my accounts of you remain pure
only on the tongue do i repel you
but beneath skin
and follicle
your image floods
the highways of blood to my clever heart

songs give me to you
leaves fall
in my passing thoughts of you
        what more dedication must you deserve

you may have slept beside
and touched me as
a wave
moves over a
lazy seal
but you did not
feel me
you were as a river
rolling down the tight
skinned bed
of my young body
only through raw desire no chosen route
rippling and current fed
you dismembered all i had
set up
to slow this
torrid flow

while you and i breathed as one
and the unseen
indents
of flesh gathered
a combined nectar of our embrace
he sighed above us

he who infiltrated the foggy mesh
of my dreams
and stole you away
from that once hidden
valley
he who has in his possession
all the juices of your soul
labeled with an iron kiss

i chose a lipstick seal

17

i imagine the smashing of your breast
then i quickly repent to save a distance from you
some nights i find i am chanting
a backwards name of your
worship
voices
later less voices
but with lips of flames
forgive me precious rose
i only want
holy rain for your bed

upon my kneeling at your root
i am exempt of any sour affairs

my life shall be short as i
kneel
forever at your rising appeal
and eventual
flight away to walk with
another
who
can
only
utter words of sweetness

18

words of my tongue
bite the ears
of my lover
and even tears
of my eyes
salt the sweetness
of her grace

and of pain
it must be
that the silence
of my soul
aches through her limbs
and beyond her immortal gaze

it is like the immense stillness
of the moon filled sea
stranding those who tempt
her
formlessness

19

with each word
forward
underneath my snail tongue
forward
i must give

what lacks is heat
blood runs cold

soon
hope whispers
through whatever
excess or abstinence
my veins will enliven
as my loins
when
inside a tender lover

the gaze
of a
newborn child

20

if life is not for giving it away
in boxes
and squeezing a little home
into a bag
and slipping across
borders with a naked gypsy
who promises
only to steal your heart
well sir what is it for
tell me
before my lunch break
is over
and i return
to feverishly
padding my bank account
with the
blood
of my
murdered promise
with interest

the resting pond

                    is unhurried
save
its own conviction

salted sprees
of the tide
fills the hunger

                    of space

in quiet groves
moves
                    a gentle yawn

still formless grace
again gentler

All forever drinking
All forever parched

22

bless this day with a
simple adjective
bless this day with a
lively verb
bless this day with a
mounting expression
bless me each day love
blow into my ears the
fibre of your woes
the down of your passions
and the sweetness of your sight

23

it's all in the eyes
your clouds
and
maps
to the sun

when you follow a wisp to its bed
will you lay with it
and mother
its children
or
do you run

who ran from you in your night
who let expire the source of your blossoming

the great winds exposed your tenderness
where father sun reddened your heart

but wilt not child
new skin grows
under the blistered fountain of your dreams

bathe it in tears as the mountain feeds the
streams and
infant pools of creation

you are being created now
just notice and open your eyes
to look upon yourself
                        in these clouds

24

i reach into humanity's roots
and tap a dreaming line of memories for your soul
some sad
some happy
mostly ones that can only
whisper in
languages beyond you
and only when you return to the soil will they
translate themselves
for i am in those whispers and must remain as
such

i do this for you but mostly for me as i am a
coward
only you will not know this
you will not know your creator or your destroyer

you will only know the handpicked spies disguised
as bees that bring you pollen while tasting you
and delivering your sweetness to my tongue

i command the wind the sparrows and the moonlight
nature allows this for it is my dream
my tortured bliss

25

you will not end
you never began

the breath you breathe
the blood you pulse
cannot be traced

    they are beyond form
    their lineage vast

and when the threads unwind at your dying
the spindles
and spools
will be revealed as but
echos
reflecting all that is
within and beyond
at once

sensing my remorse
i reach out to you
not knowing you
i imagine you
creating lashes
kneecaps
and a scar where
as a child
you scraped your hip chasing birds

i touch the shadowy lines of your laughter
the slow engrained lines of your sadness
where
above
your tears spoke to the sun
and then vanished
before being caught in the minute floodways of
your face

not words
on the page

there's no fire in my heart no bliss from whence
to start
when the dreams of youth have not yet flowered
and time through seconds my life's devoured

is there hope inside this page
a key to light
the spirit's cage

from the mind and ego same
mixtures dwell
to fuel this game

of love so pale and
courted muse
i do not tire
and still i use

the aging frame
hair eyes and tongue
ascending that tower
rung by rung

to lonesome flight
in air i steal
a gaze of wonder
set in distant appeal

your golden squint
from
sun's decree
i like you
am never free

so when the tarp and blankets
lift
into my cave
the light shall drift
and holding still in my egoic cast
a weightless boy
to rock held
fast

28

can't i burn in your madness
be torn apart
in your orbit
i open your eyes
not to see
not to find
or to be seen
or be found
but to know
but to adorn

i melt on your altar
i explode at your opening
you are an echo in smoke
naked behind the shroud
and you are nothing
you tell nothing of the dance but present the
song
the only song
the mother of all loves
the pain inside
the joyous shiver that freezes me now

so can't i burn for once

and eternally

so that the ashes may mount

and be built upon with temples to Venus

wherein

my children of embers

may worship under your sun

blown over and struck by snow with crystals in my
eyes
while the prairie and her guarding trees raise a
last triumphant valley for my lone rocky voice

drift me over and burrow in my intestine
and plant in my roots
and build on my bones
and dig up my ashes
and spread me on fire
and smoke my red embers
and then celebrate my death

30

did you run from the fire too soon
before the flames melted your flesh
and tendons
and organs
and bones
only to reveal
the secret
the truth
of you

did you turn and run towards a glimmer
a shadow of your dreams
an oasis of magic

i imagine you did
for i am in the turning
and the stepping
look at me
my face half scorched
will you call to me and stop your running
and
join me at the ceremony where all will be
revealed
and you will forget
your thirst
your hunger
and you will become
the wine
the bread
all at once
as you burn and burn for others who come
and turn
and turn again
to burn themselves away
so that they may return without want or desire
only ashes that spread far wider than

hope
or coin

i live in the dissonant

in reach of the tonic

the heroic

muted by withholding

frozen in expression

witness to my limits

enslaved to the immediate

born into a muddy brew

the perennial muddy lotus

skewed

and muttering

hints of passion

and of inspirations kiss

lost on the slopes of creation

only whispering at my exaltation

crying without words

but with tears of potential lost

i fragment at your feet

willing to serve

32

i want to write myself out of existence

            and allow the river to exalt in

emptiness

i dance these words onto page

                to silence the heart melting hum

over

        and

                                    over

                they softly inscribe

                            like terrible

            beats of a drum

33

When you wake, wake!
Whether to golden images of him or her, wake!
Whether to raging mimics slicing the streets,
wake!
Whether to an itch a thousand leagues down, wake!
Whether to the disquieted urgings of your gut,
wake!
Whether to the crash of garbage from the
discarded self, wake!
Whether to the moist reflections of your pulsing
veins, wake!
Whether to the sirens blazing to a birth of
injury, wake!

Wake and dance the ecstatic dance

Wake and sculpt the new David of your form

Wake and rekindle the ancient flame

Wake and sing until you stumble on truth

Wake and weep for all souls in torment

Wake and climb to the height of your terrors

Wake and gather all the spiders in the moonlight

Wake and let loose your serpents of distrust

Wake and proclaim your love from the rooftop

Wake and stand naked in the courtyard of your
virtue

Wake and be still by the cliffs and valleys

Wake and return to the womb of The Mother
Wake so you may sink in the absence of the sea

Wake so you may carry no poison to the feast
Wake so you may journey into the telling of our
slumber

the stream does not wait for itself
nor do the awakened quench her thirst

the muddy flow from the glacier
empties and fills
itself
and the clear lake
of its waking
below

34

here i am on the edge of it all
cut from the past and sheathed in the future
my naming unknown and my purpose hidden

words spill from the bodied soul
only hints and shadows for what can the body know

the body knows its consequence of birth
the soul wields the sword

as the words fall they are pierced and rendered
into nothing coming to rest on one side or the
other

at play on this razor edge of The Way my body
struggles for balance while the soul dances and
jumps

in dreams the body retreats and the soul and mind
begin their dance

edges widen and the game expands

but in the wakened world of fleeting hopes and
rooted desires the edge is thin and always
injuring

and the blood that spills on its descending sides
projects the images of our dreams and the earthly
drama

so what choice do i have but to bleed

bleed the body of all
giving it away to the nothingness below

i hold to everything now which quickens the flow
for this death on the edge is all we really know
but do not know

and i bleed for you and for him
and i am bled like the lamb bleating
but willing to be brought to the altar for its
final worship and cry into the earthbound night

at your death do i sigh or cry or weep
at your death do i hold or push or run

no at your death i will be
i will stand breathing like a tree
all that is and was is still at hand
all that hides behind the moon is still inside
truth

at your death i shall wander naked into the
lushness of our mother
at your death i shall present myself at her bosom

yes i will drink you at the rivers edge
yes i will bathe in you among moss and mud
yes i will sway and droop with your eternal
breeze
yes i will follow you on the path of stones and
cosmic dirt

before you
around you
beneath you
above you

i will be in you as you dance in me

at your death
the whispers
in your vanishing
the glimmers

in the closest touch
    i do not reach you
dissolving atoms
and particles of love
find
        an absent embrace
in a hot breath of passion
my blood finds no heat
for
isolated
shadows and stacked lines of letters
            brings not flames but hopes
            and dreams are not pregnant
                with flesh
                and lips
            and arching strands
                but weighted
            by the orbit of moons
            and dust of the gods
        who shake from their dreams
                my prayers
            and old schemes
                of love
                and
            adventure

i did not dream of your tearing

from me

i lived it

a momentary terror at the deaths

to come at your

feet

there in the warmly lit

cave

i descended

to

your

voice

calling me to my own pyre

beckoning me to the tombs

depth

in a circle of sunlight i shivered

as an ancient to his demigod

and was slain at the blade of your emergence

cosmic lover
dancing the dream of our courtship
through the eternal dust
of my charred soul

you are not gone
for i am you
and we circle
each other
along the cavernous path
away
and towards
the centre
where we are
split
and torn
from within
as the eternal
struggle for oneness
that lies inherent and virginal
disrupts the sleeping gods and mothers of
the source
spoken throughout the
entrances
and passageways
from
without

our golden vessel is swallowed in a watery blur
of sunlight
as i descend
cast off by your beautiful and fearsome storm

again through my purposeful fated death you shall
sail on into your many gentle deaths

but

before our hearts whisper the end
let me bring forth the gems of the deep

even in your deafening distance my underworld
currents will move your souls immortal compass

beyond the abyss i harken to you in
sunless rituals of moist stone and urchins
relaying the secrets of your freedom
and the songs of your eternal paradise

while your limbs pupils and flesh
are but molecules of light in the scripture of my
endurance
the melody of our timeless heart pulses gently
and instructs
the oration of my subterraneous
soul journey back to you

in another body
in another time
under transformed constellations
within the same formless caverns
of never ending dying
journeys

40

hot pincers extended
black hair smoked
ash and teary
he covers her in the blame
of a thousand cloaks and in the stains of
bleeding passion

king or slave
bread-maker or sorcerer
their arrows true and
mortal
her heart a straw animal
a justified feast
have we eaten
have we pursued
this fawn of the pulsating meadow

her tongue severed and burnt
her side punctured
oh The Magdalene
of our caverns and caves
return to us
emerge voiceless and beautiful
your gowns we may clean
your feet we may wash

to prepare you for the lifetimes of searching

chasing your voice

through your body and its pains and loves

birthing

and

being

birthed

41

even as the sun penetrates all that is
and cannot be seen
and plants extinguish all matter
in spasms of survival
and insects
hoard into the nucleus
and are squeezed out
and darkness spits sparks
of illumination
to be felt
or feared
you will not be hidden

i see through the sun
i am the swallower of the
extinguished
and the teller in the night
even now as you disappear
behind words
i read of your journey
and sing songs to your
hideout

42

i am not a quiet dinner
nor am i a straight line on any day
nor a one way home at 5 o'clock
nor a porcelain bath not i

i am not the ride home with
groceries in the back
nor coloured paintings hung one night
nor a portrait of us or them
nor a familiar cuddle not i

i am air brushed aside at the turning of a page

i am the warmth within you when you read a moving
phrase
i am longing
i am a shoreline

i am a tree of birds
                    that
        sways
            and
                empties

43

breathe into the dying breath

of mouths hung open
          in silent exit

breathe into the dying breath

that escapes with our sight
          and unspoken dreams

breathe into the dying breath

the breath that dies not
          but incarnates us all

breathe into the dying breath

we are the light
          we are the light

EPILOGUE

slipping between my fingers you disappear
and i cannot name you
as you
only as me
my dream
my illusion
my safety
for i am a coward
and i create
only that which i can make

vanish

ABOUT THE AUTHOR

Markus Adam

Never completely happy never completely sad
Markus is an emotional through-line of life, a
tree leaning beyond its base, a wet heart in a
scorched desert weeping tears of contentment and
despair. He is all things at once, but still a
momentary pinpoint of self.

Markus is a quester and a maker of meaning. He
has found his tribe among diverse communities
seeking mentors and allies along the way. Drawing
on the wisdom of spirit and the voracity of mind
he moves forward along the thin edge of a moment
forever failing and succeeding. Words and images
descend from what he calls The Mystic Mother. His
role is simply to harness and enliven them on the
page.